A Note to Parents and Teachers

SAINSBURY'S READING SCHEME is a compelling new reading programme for children, designed in conjunction with leading literacy experts, including Cliff Moon M.Ed., Honorary Fellow of the University of Reading. Cliff Moon has spent many years as a teacher and teacher educator specializing in reading and has written more than 140 books for children and teachers. He reviews regularly for teachers' journals.

Beautiful illustrations and superb full-colour photographs combine with engaging, easy-to-read stories to offer a fresh approach to each subject. Each book in the SAINSBURY'S READING SCHEME programme is guaranteed to capture a child's interest while developing his or her reading skills, general knowledge, and love of reading.

The five levels of the programme are aimed at different reading abilities, enabling you to choose the books that are exactly right for your child:

Yellow Level – Learning to read
Green Level – Beginning to read
Gold Level – Beginning to read alone
Ruby Level – Reading alone
Sapphire Level – Proficient readers

The "normal" age at which a child begins to read can be anywhere from three to eight years old, so these levels are only a general guideline.

No matter which level you select, you can be sure that you are helping your child learn to read, then read to learn!

First published 2012 by Kingfisher
an imprint of Macmillan Children's Books
a division of Macmillan Publishers Limited
20 New Wharf Road, London N1 9RR
Basingstoke and Oxford
Associated companies throughout the world
www.panmacmillan.com

Series editor: Heather Morris
Literacy consultant: Hilary Horton

ISBN: 978-0-7534-3829-9
Copyright © Macmillan Publishers Ltd 2012

9 8 7 6 5 4 3 2 1

1TR/0714/WKT/UG/105MA

A CIP catalogue record for this book is available from
the British Library.

Printed in China

Picture credits
The Publisher would like to thank the following for permission to reproduce their material. Every care has
been taken to trace copyright holders. However, if there have been unintentional omissions or failure to trace
copyright holders, we apologize and will, if informed, endeavour to make corrections in any future edition
(t = top, b = bottom, c = centre, r = right, l = left):
Cover Shutterstock (SS)/Ammit, Nature Picture Library/Martin Dohrn, Nature PL/Phil Savoie, Alamy/Edward
Parker; Pages 1 Shutterstock/ Boonchuay Promjiam; 3 Shutterstock/ Dirk Ercken; 4–5 SS/szefel; 5l Alamy/
Frans Lanting; 5r SS/worldswildlifewonders; 7tr Science Photo Library (SPL)/Jacques Jangouxl; 10cl Alamy/
Shorelark Nigel Downer; 10–11b Photolibrary/OSF; 12 Frank Lane Picture Agency (FLPA)/Ingo Arndt/Minden;
13b Alamy/Bruce Farnsworth; 15 FLPA/Piotr Naskrecki/Minden; 16 SS/ecoventurestravel; 17tr FLPA/Frans
Lanting; 20 SS/worldswildlifewonders; 21 FLPA/Piotr Naskrecki/Minden; 23 SS/Henrik Lehnerer; 24 Nature
PL/Nick Gordon; 25 FLPA/Norbert Wu/Minden; 26b Nature PL/Kim Taylor; 27b Nature PL/Kim Taylor;
28 FLPA/Frans Lanting; 29 FLPA/Thomas Marent/Minden; 30 SS/Colette3; 31t FLPA/Filip de Nooyer/Minden;
32 SS/Fikmik; 33t FLPA/Imagebroker; 33b Ardea/Nick Gordeon; 34 SS/miorenz; 35t FLPA/Mike Lane;
35b FLPA/Pete Oxford/Minden; 37t Ardea/Andrew Zvoznikov; 37b Nature Picture Library/Martin Dohrn;
38 Nature Picture Library/Pete Oxford; 39t FLPA/D.Donne Bryant; 39b FLPA/Imagebroker; 40 Nature PL/Phil
Savoie; 41t Nature PL/Luiz Claudio Marigo; 41b SS/Frontpage; 42 SS/szefel; 43t SS/Dmitry Kosterev;
43b Alamy/Edward Parker; 44–45 SS/Frontpage; 45t Alamy/Simon Rawles; 45b SS/Howard Sandler.
All other images Kingfisher Artbank.

Sainsbury's
Reading Scheme

Sapphire Level
Proficient readers

Rainforests

Written by Chris Oxlade

KINGFISHER

What is a rainforest?

Rainforests are thick, lush forests with trees that stay green all year round. All rainforests have a lot of rain and are very damp. Tropical rainforests grow in areas of the world called the **tropics** where it is also very warm. The **climate** is perfect for plants and rainforest trees to grow very tall and close together. Tropical rainforests are full of wildlife. Half of all the plants and animals in the world live here.

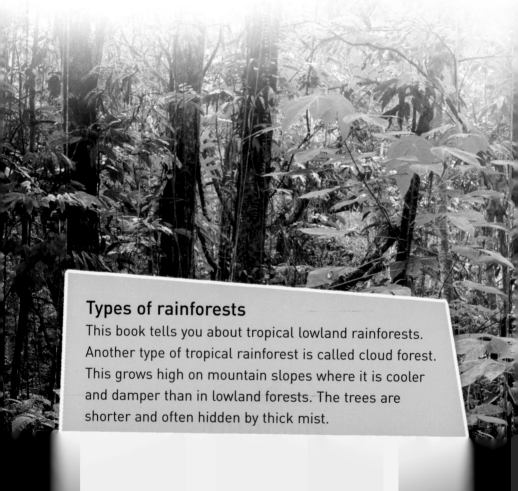

Types of rainforests

This book tells you about tropical lowland rainforests. Another type of tropical rainforest is called cloud forest. This grows high on mountain slopes where it is cooler and damper than in lowland forests. The trees are shorter and often hidden by thick mist.

In rainforests most of the wildlife lives high in the treetops. This part of the forest is called the **canopy**. Here there is plenty of rain, wind and sunlight for flowers, fruit and leaves to grow and attract wildlife. The branches and leaves of the canopy can be so thick they make the rainforest underneath shady and dark.

Macaws belong to the parrot family. They live in the Amazon rainforests.

Tree frogs have sticky pads on their toes to help them climb.

Where are rainforests?

There are tropical rainforests on either side of the **Equator**. This is an imaginary line that circles the middle of the world like a belt. The tropics are areas north and south of the Equator. There are no seasons here and the weather is hot and wet all the time. The tropics give their name to tropical rainforests.

Nearly half of all tropical rainforests are in South America. The next biggest rainforest area is in Africa. Other tropical rainforests are found in South-east Asia and Australia.

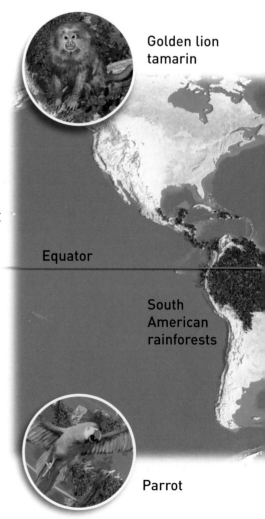

Golden lion tamarin

Equator

South American rainforests

Parrot

The tropics: This map shows the tropical rainforests (in dark green) in a band around the Equator. The Equator is half way between the North and South Poles.

The world's largest rainforest is the Amazon rainforest (pictured right) in South America. It is almost as big as the whole of the USA. The world's biggest river, the Amazon, runs through it.

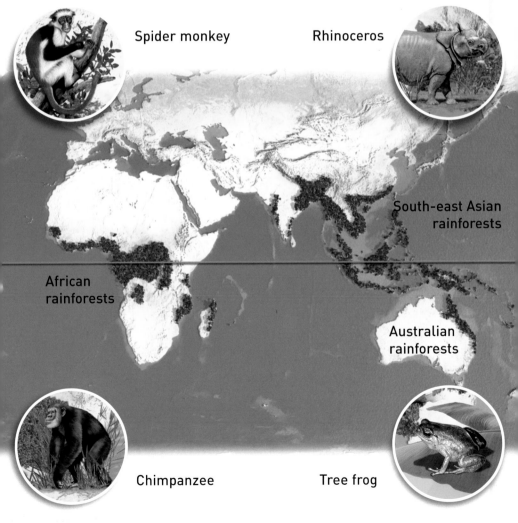

Spider monkey

Rhinoceros

South-east Asian rainforests

African rainforests

Australian rainforests

Chimpanzee

Tree frog

Inside a tropical rainforest

Imagine you are walking on a soft pile of dead leaves in a dim light. You pass between giant tree trunks covered in twisted vines. Insects scuttle along old branches and dead leaves. There are lots of ferns. You are on the rainforest floor, where it is quiet and still and also very hot and sticky.

Above you are the branches of small trees and bushes. High above them is the giant green roof of the forest. Very little sunlight, wind or rain gets through this thick layer.

Here are flocks of brilliantly coloured parrots and groups of leaping monkeys. You might see a gibbon swinging through the branches. This is the busiest and noisiest part of the rainforest.

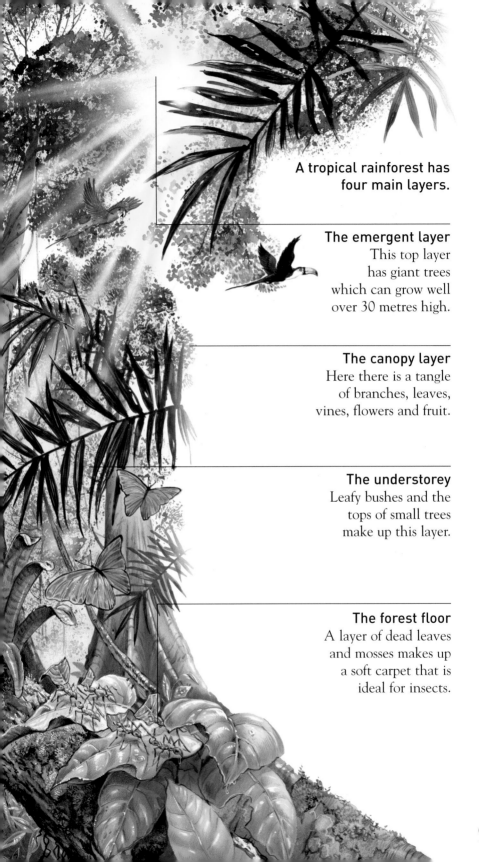

A tropical rainforest has
four main layers.

The emergent layer
This top layer
has giant trees
which can grow well
over 30 metres high.

The canopy layer
Here there is a tangle
of branches, leaves,
vines, flowers and fruit.

The understorey
Leafy bushes and the
tops of small trees
make up this layer.

The forest floor
A layer of dead leaves
and mosses makes up
a soft carpet that is
ideal for insects.

9

Life in the treetops

The tallest trees in the **emergent layer** of the rainforest tower ten metres or more above the canopy. At this height they feel the full force of the rain, the sun and the wind. They have small, waxy leaves that help to stop them drying out. The wind blows away some of the leaves, but more grow to take their place. Wind also helps to spread the trees' seeds through the rest of the forest.

The blue morpho's brilliant blue wings can be 15cm across.

Gibbons have long arms for swinging from branch to branch. They can travel three metres in a single swing.

The branches of the tallest trees can spread as wide as a football pitch. They are the home of soaring eagles searching for **prey** and noisy gangs of high-flying parrots. Butterflies and bats fly in this top layer and monkeys live there too. Gibbons are the only apes to spend their whole lives up in the trees.

In the canopy

The busiest and noisiest part of the rainforest is the canopy layer. It is made up of tangled leaves and branches. The leaves are mostly smooth, oval-shaped and end in a point so the rain drips off them. Some sunlight, breezes and rain come through the canopy and allow fruits and flowers to grow.

In the tropics, every canopy tree releases huge amounts of water into the air. The moisture helps to form the thick clouds that hang over most rainforests. The clouds keep the rainforest warm and damp.

This blue-headed parrot has green feathers on its body, wings and tail. It has a high, squeaky call.

More animals live in the canopy
than anywhere else in the rainforest.
It is home to all sorts of monkeys – the
acrobats of the rainforest. Birds, snakes and
tree frogs also live here. Many animals can
leap or glide from one tree to another.

Hidden world
Scientists know more about
the surface of the moon than
they know about the emergent
layer and canopy. They build
aerial walkways and fly in
hot air balloons in order to
study this hidden world.

In the understorey

The rainforest **understorey** is humid, which means warm and wet. The understorey is also dark because very little sunlight reaches it through the canopy. The plants here **adapt** to life in the shade. They grow large, dark green leaves to catch the little light there is. These plants do not grow more than four metres tall.

Liana

Morpho butterfly

Yellow-banded poison dart frog

Lobster claw plant

There is very little wind, so plants rely on insects and animals to **pollinate** their flowers. There are more insects here than anywhere else in the rainforest.

Plants such as ferns and palms soak up the moisture on the forest floor. Lianas are climbing plants that grow well here too. They climb up other plants and trees. Many animals use them as ropes and bridges to reach the understorey to look for food.

Vine

Tree frog

This diving lizard likes the warm, wet conditions of the rainforest.

The understorey is full of small trees, as well as lianas, vines and plants with large leaves.

15

On the rainforest floor

The forest floor is the lowest layer of the rainforest and hardly any plants grow here. It is too dark for grass to grow. The ground is covered with dead leaves and twigs that have fallen from above. The largest rainforest animals, such as tapirs and capybaras, search for roots and **tubers**. Small creatures such as millipedes, scorpions, spiders and earthworms find food here.

Many types of **fungi** grow here, helping to rot the fallen leaves. The rotting leaves provide **nutrients** which the trees and plants take up through their roots to help them grow. All these nutrients are in the top five centimetres of the soil and they help the tallest trees to grow in the very thin soil.

Tree frog

Mushrooms are fungi that eat or break down rotting trees and plants.

Trunks and roots

Some of the largest tree trunks are as wide as a car. Many tree trunks have huge roots called **buttress** roots. These stretch across the forest floor and take up water and nutrients from the soil to feed the tree.

Capybaras are related to guinea pigs, but they are much bigger – about a metre long.

Ants

Buttress root

Tapir

Not much light reaches the forest floor because of the thick canopy of leaves above.

Blue poison dart frog

A rainforest river

The biggest river in the world is the Amazon. It gives its name to the Amazon rainforest – the world's largest tropical rainforest. More than 1,000 smaller rivers and streams flow into the Amazon.

The main river is more than 6,500 kilometres long. It floods many parts of the rainforest every year. The river is home to some amazing creatures, including sharp-toothed piranha fish.

Many animals eat the plants that grow on the river banks, but there are dangerous hunters in rainforest rivers.

Piranha

Caiman

18

Piranha fish hunt in packs and some **species** can be dangerous to humans. Other fish include giant catfish and electric eels that release a dangerous electric shock.

Long-nosed Amazon river dolphins search the muddy river bottom for food. Manatees are slow-moving **mammals** that browse in rivers, looking for water plants. They are also called sea cows. Alligators called caimans live along the river banks and in flooded swamps, snapping up turtles, fish and even capybaras.

Capybara

Electric eel

Animals of the rainforest

The three-toed sloth hangs upside down from its powerful, hook-like claws and sleeps for as much as 16 hours a day. It may be the world's slowest-moving animal. The sloth stays in the trees eating leaves for most of the time, and climbs down to the ground to go to the toilet just once a week! Tiny plants grow on its fur and turn it green. This helps the sloth to hide from its enemies and its slow speed makes it difficult to spot.

This young sloth is gripping the tree with its claws as it climbs slowly upwards.

Howler monkeys eat a lot of leaves and then spend most of the day resting. They move slowly, crawling up into the sunshine to warm their bodies after a cold night. Their deep howls can be heard many kilometres away.

Many rainforest monkeys and apes live high up in the trees. Some, such as gibbons, never come down to the ground. They live in large family groups, howling, shrieking and barking. They are acrobats, swinging, gliding and jumping from branch to branch. Most monkeys have tails which they use like an extra arm to swing about and pick up food.

Brilliant birds

More types of bird live in the tropical rainforest than anywhere else in the world. One of the smallest birds on the planet, the bee hummingbird, lives here. It is about as long as your finger.

Hummingbirds can beat their wings 12,000 times a minute while they hover and suck out nectar from flowers with their long beaks. They are the only birds that can fly backwards.

A hummingbird can stick out its tongue beyond the tip of its bill to reach the nectar inside flowers.

Scarlet macaws are very brightly coloured. Like all parrots, they have sharp claws for climbing along branches and grasping food.

Beautiful, brightly coloured parrots screech and flap in the canopy. Scarlet macaws are the largest parrots and they have a metre-long tail. They clamber through the branches to break open nuts and fruit with their powerful beaks. The largest bird in the treetops is the harpy eagle. Its wings stretch over two metres and it can snatch a monkey in its strong claws.

Beaky bird

Toucans live in the tropical rainforests of Central and South America. They nest in tree holes with other members of their noisy treetop family. Toucans eat tropical fruits and nuts, as well as large insects, baby birds and lizards.

The toucan's long, brilliantly coloured beak is hollow. It uses it to reach fruit growing on branches that are too thin and weak for it to stand on.

A toucan's beak is made of the same material as our fingernails.

A toucan can even use its beak to pull baby birds from deep inside their nests, and eat them. It can hold a nut with one foot and then use its strong beak to crack it open. A toucan's beak gets in the way when it flies, so the bird usually leaps from one tree to another with a few clumsy wing beats.

A toucan's huge beak helps to keep the bird cool. Toucans (like other birds) cannot sweat.

Insect armies

Thousands of tiny creatures such as beetles, ants and woodlice scurry about the forest floor feeding on the rotting leaves and fungi. Many insects, such as ants and termites, live together in **colonies** which are organized like armies.

Leaf-cutter ants make an amazing army. They bite off bits of leaf and carry them back to their enormous underground nest. There they chew the leaves thoroughly and then bring the chewed remains back up from their stomachs for fungi to grow on. The ants then eat this fungi. You could say they grow their own food.

The female worker ants carry pieces of leaf back to the nest to chew.

Worker ants carry the leaves. They are all female and they work amazingly hard. Each piece of leaf weighs several times as much as an ant. The workers carry the pieces very fast over long distances.

Masses of ants

More than 50 different types of ant can live in an area of rainforest as small as half a square metre.

King of the rainforest

Danger lurks at every level of a tropical rainforest. Animals on the ground must watch out for the biggest cat in the rainforest, the jaguar. The jaguar likes to prowl along tree branches, searching the forest floor for mice or larger animals such as monkeys, tapirs and deer. This big cat moves very quietly on padded paws.

The jaguar's spotted coat helps it to blend into the rainforest shadows so it can creep up on its prey.

It swims and climbs trees well. A jaguar hunts alone and can hook out fish from the river with a paw.

A jaguar will even fight an alligator and its powerful jaws can cut through a turtle's shell. These cats usually hunt at night and they have excellent eyesight. Jaguars rest and sleep in the trees, often with a leg or tail hanging over a branch.

The jaguar hunts monkeys, such as this squirrel monkey, in the lower branches of trees.

Jaguars in danger

Jaguars once roamed the rainforests freely, using trees as cover. Today they are in danger of disappearing as rainforests are cleared. The animals are also hunted for their fur and by farmers who are afraid they will kill their cattle.

Deadly snakes

Snakes are some of the deadliest animals in a tropical rainforest. Many snakes catch frogs and other small animals on the forest floor and kill them with their poisonous fangs. Other snakes slide between the branches or wrap themselves around a tree, waiting to pounce on their prey.

Some snakes squeeze their victims to death. An anaconda can crush a caiman to death and then swallow it whole. It may take several days to digest the animal and while it is doing this the snake can hardly move. The female anaconda is one of the world's biggest, longest snakes and weighs as much as a horse. This snake is not poisonous.

The yellow anaconda, like all snakes, can swim. Its eyes and nostrils are on top of its head so it can see when it hides just under the water.

Snakes are often hard to spot. The bright green scaly skin of this snake (left) blends in with the surrounding plants and trees, so it is well hidden. Here it winds round a branch and curls down to catch a chick from the bird's nest below.

Rainforest animals such as chameleons use **camouflage** to avoid being caught and eaten by snakes.

Hairy spiders and scary vampires

There are many strange animals in the rainforest. Tarantulas are huge spiders, as big as your hand. The world's biggest spider is the goliath tarantula, which is as wide as a dinner plate. It is also called the bird-eating spider because it hunts small birds or young chicks in their nests.

Most tarantulas are black or brown and hairy. Many hunt using their sharp bite rather than spinning webs to catch food.

Tarantulas hunt at night. They are covered in thick hairs which sense their prey moving in the dark. These **predators** use their huge poisonous fangs to catch other spiders, insects, lizards and frogs.

Jumping spiders can spring 50 times their body length in one leap, but they still get caught and eaten by tarantulas.

A thousand different types of bats live in the Amazon rainforest, but only one type feeds on blood. It is called the vampire bat. The bat hunts at night. It lands close to a sleeping animal, and then walks up to it. The bat bites into the animal and then drinks its blood.

The hairy-legged vampire bat has very sharp teeth to bite into its prey without waking it up.

Other rainforest animals

Some of the strangest mammals **forage** for food on the forest floor. Armadillos have scaly body armour that protects their backs from big cats such as jaguars. Giant armadillos are as big as sheep. They use their powerful claws to dig for insects and worms.

The armadillo has a hard outer body armour made of bone that protects it from enemies.

Capybaras are the biggest **rodents** in the world. They are the same size as pigs and are related to guinea pigs. They have partly webbed feet which make them good swimmers. On land they are awkward and waddle along like ducks. They live in groups.

Tapirs have a strange nose that looks like a short elephant trunk.

Tapirs are **timid** animals that feed on leaves and fruit at night. During the day they hide in the understorey. Tapirs swim very well and can stay under water for many minutes to hide from human or animal hunters.

The ocelot is now endangered because people hunt it for its beautiful, patterned fur.

The ocelot is a wildcat hunter with sharp, scissor-like teeth. It catches frogs, lizards, monkeys and armadillos. An ocelot tears its food to pieces and swallows it whole; it does not chew.

Rainforest peoples

Different peoples live in rainforest villages along the banks of the rivers. In these villages local tribes live in the same way they have lived for thousands of years. Among the native peoples are the Kayapo and Yanomani Indians of the Amazon.

Yanomani Indians have shown scientists where to find useful plants for medicine.

Native peoples live in harmony with the rainforests – hunting animals, fishing in the rivers, gathering fruit, nuts and insects and growing vegetables in small plots. Their food, clothing, medicines and shelter all come from the forest.

Parts of the tropical rainforest are flooded for several months at a time, so people build their houses on stilts. They cut down smaller trees to make dugout canoes so they can travel around on the water.

A Kayapo boy from the Amazon rainforest. The Kayapo Indians farm and gather wild fruits, nuts and leaves from the forest.

Many peoples still take part in ancient ceremonies and wear face paint and bright, feathered headdresses.

More recently, other people have moved to the rainforest from the crowded big cities where it is hard to earn money. These people clear the forest so they can grow food.

Living with the rainforest

The people who have always lived in the rainforest know that the soil there is thin. They cannot grow crops for more than a few years on one piece of land.

People clear a small patch by cutting down plants and setting fire to them. Then they grow crops to eat and to feed their farm animals. They plant sweet potatoes, maize and beans, as well as fruit and palm trees, but they leave the big trees standing. They farm the land for a few years, then let rainforest plants grow again.

This man is chopping open the hard outer shells to take out the Brazil nuts inside.

A woman picks ripe berries from a coffee bush.

Some tribes also gather wild fruits, nuts and leaves from the forest and plants for medicine. They know what to look for and what to avoid. Some rainforest people sell what they grow and catch in markets, including coffee, cotton and fish. They also cut vines and palm leaves to make twine, nets, baskets and sleeping mats.

Rubber from trees
Many people work in the rubber industry. They drain a sticky white liquid called **latex** from wild rubber trees. This is used to make things such as tyres.

Workers cut a slit in the tree bark and collect the latex in a can.

Rainforests in danger

Vast areas of tropical rainforest are destroyed every day. This is partly because companies cut down trees to sell as timber. The hardwood is used to make furniture and paper. Other companies clear areas of forest so that cattle can graze there, then they sell the meat as beef around the world. Some companies destroy areas of the rainforest so they can dig out valuable minerals lying under the ground.

Many animals, such as this tree frog, are in danger of **extinction** if the rainforest is destroyed.

Today, there are roads running through many rainforests. Giant trucks carry logs, minerals and farm animals along the roads. People build towns for the workers who come to live there. Companies build dams and pipelines which may **pollute** the land and the water. Many local tribes are forced to leave.

Farmers clear the forests so they can plant huge fields of soya beans and other crops. These are fed to huge herds of cattle kept on even bigger ranches. Much of the beef from the cattle goes into burgers and pet food.

Rainforest trees are cut down or burnt to turn the land into plantations or cattle ranches.

41

Rainforest resources

Tropical rainforests are home to a huge range
of wildlife and plants – more than anywhere else
on Earth. Yet rainforests cover only a tiny part of
our planet. When rainforests disappear, so do the
amazing animals and plants that live in them.

Tropical rainforest plants give us many medicines and drugs, including those used to fight cancer.

Tropical rainforests are sometimes called 'the lungs of
the planet'. This is because the millions of rainforest
trees and plants take in **carbon dioxide** and give
out oxygen, which is the gas we need to breathe.
Humans are pumping out too much carbon dioxide
from power stations, factories and cars.

A single rainforest tree is home to more types of ants than there are in the whole of the UK.

Too much carbon dioxide in the Earth's **atmosphere** leads to **global warming**, which can change our climate. When people cut down rainforests, that leaves fewer trees to turn the carbon dioxide into oxygen. This makes the problem of global warming worse.

This pretty plant, the rosy periwinkle, is used to make drugs which treat some types of cancer. It grows in the rainforests on Madagascar.

Rainforest future

As you read this book, tropical rainforests are shrinking. Every second a piece of rainforest the size of a football field is destroyed or damaged. The future of the world's rainforests is very uncertain.

Rainforests are cut down for timber and to make large farms to grow crops and raise cattle. Companies which mine **minerals**, build new roads, towns and pipelines all destroy areas of rainforest.

Fair trade companies work with local people to protect them and the **environment**.

Today there are many **campaigns** to protect rainforests. One scheme allows **reserves** or parks where no one can build or clear trees to create large farms. Everyone can help rainforests by buying fair trade bananas, coffee and cocoa, as well as wood and paper sold by companies which do not destroy the forests.

Rainforests need clean, flowing rivers and regular flooding to nourish the soil.

Rainforests are home to wonderful wildlife, such as the very rare golden lion tamarin.

45

Glossary

adapt To change in order to survive.

aerial walkways Tree branches in the canopy, or man-made rope bridges.

atmosphere The layer of air around the Earth.

buttress A root which often grows from a trunk and helps to keep a tree standing.

camouflage A colour or pattern that matches an animal's surroundings and makes it difficult to see.

campaign Action taken by a group of people to protect something, such as rainforests and the animals that live in them.

canopy The rainforest's 'roof', or layer of high branches.

carbon dioxide A gas that is released into the atmosphere. Cutting down the trees that trap the gas leads to global warming.

climate The general weather in an area.

colonies Groups of plants and animals living together.

emergent layer The tallest trees in a rainforest, above the canopy.

environment The surroundings in which an animal or plant lives, including the other animals and plants that live there.

Equator An imaginary line around the middle of the world midway between the Poles.

extinction When an animal or plant species dies out completely.

forage To search for food.

fungi Living things such as mushrooms and toadstools, that are not plants or animals.

global warming A rise in temperatures on Earth, which can lead to problems for the environment, wildlife and people.

latex A milky substance that comes from rubber trees.

mammal An animal that feeds its young on milk from its body.

minerals Substances that are part of the Earth's rock and soil.

nutrient Food that plants and animals need to absorb to grow and stay healthy.

pollinate To transfer pollen from one flower to another, part of the way plants make new plants.

pollute To poison the air, water or soil.

predator An animal that hunts other animals, or prey, for food.

prey Animals hunted and caught by other animals for food.

reserves Protected places.

rodent A mammal with long front teeth such as a guinea pig.

species A group of plants or animals that breed together to produce young.

timid Shy.

tropics Areas of the world near the Equator where it is always warm and often wet.

tuber The swollen stem of a plant, which grows underground.

understorey The area above the forest floor where bushes and young trees grow close together.

Index

Sainsbury's
Reading Scheme

CERTIFICATE
of Reading

My name is

_____

I have read

_____

Date

_____